A Tortoise Keeper's Diary

by Ellie Irving
Illustrated by Nina de P...

OXFORD

UNIVERSITY PRESS

Friday, 1st May

Dad and I passed the pet shop again today. I tried to drag him inside.

"Sorry, Poppy," Dad said. "You know the rules."

I do know the rules. One of the rules is that I can't have a pet.

I stared through the window.

Inside, there were shelves of fish tanks, shiny dog leads, and rabbit hutches as big as my bed.

Staring through a window is the closest I'll ever come to having a pet. It's not fair.

I've got asthma, so fur makes me wheeze. Sometimes I wheeze so badly I have to use my inhaler.

Being fair means treating everyone in the same way. Why did Poppy think that it wasn't fair that she couldn't have a pet?

Here's a list of all the animals I would love to own but never will ...

- Dogs, cats, rabbits, hamsters: asthma
- Chickens: not enough space on the balcony of our flat; neighbours might complain about the clucking
- Fish: no fur, but not much fun: you can't cuddle a fish or take it for walks
- Crocodile: wouldn't fit in the bath; might eat Dad.

Just then, a lady with three dogs came out of the shop.

Dad put his arm round my shoulders. "Let's go, before you start sneezing," he said. "Why don't we make a cake when we get home?"

I knew he was trying to distract me, but making a cake is never going to beat getting a pet, is it?

Saturday, 2nd May

You'll never guess what happened this morning! Nelson from next door has asked me to look after his pet tortoise, Bertie. It's amazing!

Nelson has been our neighbour for ages. He's always smiling and has curly grey hair.

Can you pretend to be Poppy saying: "It's amazing"?

I've done some research on tortoises. Here are my top three facts:

1. A group of tortoises is called a 'creep'.
2. Tortoises don't have teeth.
3. Tortoises can live up to the age of 150.

Bertie is a small type of tortoise called a Hermann's tortoise.

"Small enough to fit in the palm of my hand," Nelson said. "Although I always use two hands to hold him."

Dad and I went to Nelson's flat this afternoon.

Nelson is going away for two weeks to visit his daughter. He can't take Bertie because his daughter has a big dog.

"Don't worry," I said. "I'll take good care of him."

I am really eager to start looking after Bertie. In fact, I can't wait!

Poppy is eager to start looking after Bertie. Can you think of another word or phrase that means the same as 'eager'?

Tortoise keeping

Tortoises need:
- **Food**: tortoise food, cabbage, watercress, dandelions and sprouts (Yuk! Bertie can have mine!)
- **Water**: Bertie will need fresh water every day.
- **Heat lamp**: make sure this is always switched on during the day. Bertie needs to be able to keep warm.

Dad and Nelson moved Bertie's 'tortoise table' into our flat.

Nelson gently lifted Bertie out and let me hold him. I stroked his shell. Bertie poked out his tongue and licked my palm. It felt rough, like sandpaper! I think it means he likes me.

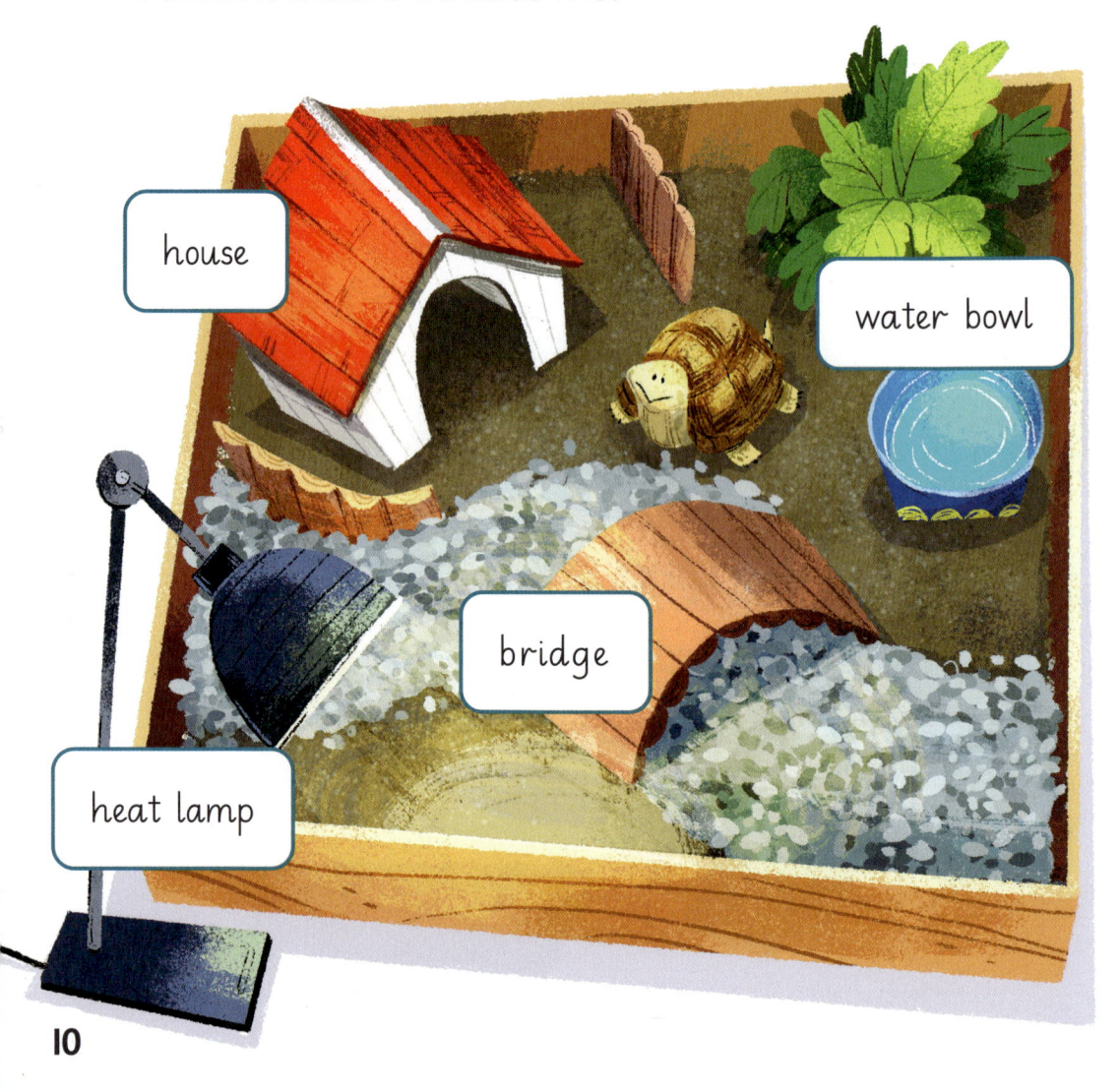

house

water bowl

bridge

heat lamp

I love looking after Bertie, but I'm a little <u>anxious</u> about it.

"Aren't you hungry?" Dad asked, when I didn't eat much at dinner.

"I'm just going to check on Bertie again," I said, heading for the tortoise table.

Dad and I peered down at Bertie. "He looks very happy," Dad said. "You're doing a great job so far."

Why might Poppy be feeling <u>anxious</u> about looking after Bertie? What words other than '<u>anxious</u>' might she use?

Wednesday, 6th May

I made a big mistake today. In the morning, I moved Bertie's bridge a bit because I thought he might like a change. When I checked on him after school, I couldn't find him! I realized he must have climbed out. I didn't know tortoises could climb!

"I can't believe I let this happen," I sobbed to Dad.

"Don't worry. He'll be in the flat somewhere," Dad said.

We checked everywhere:
- under the sofa
- behind the curtains in the hall
- under the rug
- inside Dad's shoes
- in the saucepan cupboard.

I even checked inside my dolls' house, just in case Bertie preferred it to his own house!

"I won't abandon the search," I said to Dad. "I must find him."

To abandon something means to give up completely. Why doesn't Poppy want to abandon the search for Bertie?

Eventually – thank goodness – we found Bertie. He was huddled up under the radiator.

"Here he is!" I shouted to Dad. "I've got him!"

I picked Bertie up and stroked his shell. "No more adventures for you," I whispered. "I'm going to be much more careful in future."

Saturday, 9th May

After Bertie's escape, I'd been thinking that maybe I wouldn't make a great pet owner after all.

Then something else happened.

Yesterday, I noticed that the bulb in Bertie's heat lamp had stopped working.

"Oh, Bertie," I said. "You'll be cold!"

"I've got a spare light bulb," Dad said.

"No, it needs to be a special bulb," I insisted.

"Then we'll just have to go to the pet shop," Dad replied.

I took a puff of my inhaler before we went inside the shop. We found the tortoise section and picked out a new bulb.

I got my pocket money out. I didn't have enough, but I really wanted to buy the bulb myself. After all, Bertie was my responsibility.

Dad said that because I felt so strongly about it, he would lend me the money and I could pay him back. I'm going to help our neighbours so that I can earn some more pocket money.

Sunday, 17th May

I've been so busy this week!

I have cleaned our kitchen, washed Mrs Wallace's car, folded Miss Clarke's laundry and watered Mr Patel's plants.

Eventually, I had enough money to pay Dad back.

In the meantime, Bertie has been having a wonderful time keeping warm under his heat lamp.

When Nelson came home, Dad told him how hard I'd worked to pay for Bertie's new bulb.

"You're a kind and thoughtful girl," Nelson said. "Thank you for taking such good care of Bertie."

I knew I had to tell him about moving Bertie's bridge and letting him escape.

I thought Nelson would be furious, but instead he said, "The main thing is, you didn't give up until you found him. I think you'd make an excellent pet owner, Poppy."

I beamed. "Thank you!"

"In fact," Nelson continued, "I wondered if you might carry on looking after Bertie? I'm going to move in with my daughter, and there's no space for Bertie there."

"What, me?" I squealed. "Really?" I was <u>amazed</u>. I couldn't believe it. My very own pet! Bertie would be perfect as he wouldn't make my asthma any worse.

"I shall miss him, though," Nelson said, sniffing.

My heart sank. Poor Nelson. It must be awful having to give up his pet. What could I do?

Can you think of another word or phrase that means the same as '<u>amazed</u>'?

Then I had an idea. "Why don't we <u>share</u> Bertie?" I said to Nelson. "Dad and I can send you pictures of him every week."

"You can visit him any time you like," Dad added.

"That sounds wonderful," Nelson said, as he stroked Bertie under the chin. "I'll feel so much happier knowing that he's gone to a good home."

How would you feel about <u>sharing</u> your pet, or favourite toy, with someone else?

Bertie's Photo Gallery

Bertie having a shower.

Bertie getting some fresh air.

Bertie having a snack.

Bertie is the best pet ever!

Read and discuss

Read and talk about the following questions.

Page 3: How do you think Poppy feels when she says: "It's not fair"? Can you say this the way Poppy might have said it?

Page 6: Can you think of a time when you might say: "It's amazing"?

Page 8: What kinds of things are you always eager to do when you get home from school?

Page 11: Have you ever felt anxious about trying something new? What was it?

Page 13: Can you think of another way of saying, "I won't abandon the search"?

Page 22: Can you describe the last thing you shared with someone else?